BOOK ANALYSIS

By Genevieve Zimantas

The House of Mirth

BY EDITH WHARTON

EDITH WHARTON 9

THE HOUSE OF MIRTH 13

SUMMARY 17

Book 1, Chapters I-VII: Betting futures
Chapters VIII-IX: Badly laid plans
Chapters X-XV: The situation worsens
Book 2, Chapters I-XIV: A love story-tragedy

CHARACTER STUDY 25

Lily Bart
Lawrence Selden
Mrs Judy Trenor
Mr Gus Trenor
Bertha Dorset
Percy Gryce
Gerty Farish
Mrs Peniston
Grace Stepney
Mr Simon Rosedale

ANALYSIS 31

Modern manners
Clothes make the woman
The burden of interiority
Absurdity and modern tragedy

FURTHER REFLECTION 39

FURTHER READING 43

EDITH WHARTON

AMERICAN NOVELIST, SHORT STORY WRITER, PLAYWRIGHT, ACTIVIST, AND DESIGNER

- **Born in New York in 1862.**
- **Died in Saint-Brice-sous-Forêt, France, in 1937.**
- **Notable works:**
  - *The Decoration of Houses* (1897), non-fiction
  - *Ethan Frome* (1911), novel
  - *The Age of Innocence* (1920), novel

Edith Wharton was born Edith Newbold Jones to a prominent New York family in the mid-19th century. She travelled throughout Europe frequently in her early life before settling permanently in France after the dissolution of her marriage. Wharton wrote nearly 20 novels and over 50 short stories as well as collections of poetry and plays and was widely recognised during her lifetime for her talent as a writer: she was the first woman to ever win the Pulitzer Prize for Fiction (for *The Age of Innocence* in 1921) and was thrice nominated for the Nobel Prize.

In addition to her literary career, Wharton was renowned for her expertise in home décor and gardening. She also distinguished herself as an important activist and advocate during the First World War (1914-1918) by raising funds for refugees fleeing German occupied Belgium, opening a workroom for unemployed women in France, and editing *The Book of the Homeless* (1915), featuring contributions by Henry James (American-British writer, 1843-1916), Joseph Conrad (Polish-British writer, 1857-1924), and an introduction by Theodore Roosevelt (American statesman, 1858-1919). For these and other efforts France made her a Chevalier of the Legion of Honour and Belgium appointed her a Chevalier of the Order of Leopold.

THE HOUSE OF MIRTH

A 20TH-CENTURY NOVEL OF MANNERS

- **Genre:** novel
- **Reference edition:** Wharton, E. (1966) *The House of Mirth*. London, Constable and Company Ltd.
- **1st edition:** 1905
- **Themes:** class, gender, wealth, love, poverty, social criticism, tragedy, self-destruction, illusion

One of Wharton's most celebrated novels, *The House of Mirth* tells the story of Lily Bart, an exceptionally beautiful woman born to a wealthy New York family but later left destitute by her father's business failures and her own idle gambling habit. Inspired by her late mother's obsession with wealth and social standing, Lily begins the novel consciously searching for a rich husband. But she is also a romantic like her father and has already let her most eligible years elapse without committing to an advantageous match.

The House of Mirth is about Lily's failed love affair with Lawrence Selden, but also about the social circumstances which lead to her tragic demise. It was well received upon first publication and sparked a passionate debate about the kind of culture it represented in its pages.

SUMMARY

BOOK 1, CHAPTERS I-VII: BETTING FUTURES

The House of Mirth begins with a chance encounter between Lily Bart and Lawrence Selden at a New York train station where the former will leave for Bellomont to stay with mutual friends. Selden announces that he is not going to Bellomont himself but agrees to keep Lily company while she waits and eventually invites her up to his nearby apartment for coffee. Lily is aware that the offer could endanger her reputation but surprises Selden by agreeing. The two have a surprisingly frank conversation about money, the realities of their respective social situations, and Lily's intention to marry rich before Lily takes her leave, refusing Selden's offer to walk her back to the station.

Lily arrives at the Trenors' summer home, but the visit does not go as planned. While Lily and Mrs Trenor, her best friend, had planned for her to entice the wealthy Mr Gryce into marriage, Lily frightens him off with her gambling debts and neglects him when Selden arrives unexpectedly, foregoing a church trip designed to win Gryce's favour for a walk and intimate conversation with Selden. Later, during a drive with Mr Trenor, Lily confesses her money troubles to her best friend's husband who promises to invest her money to secure great rewards.

CHAPTERS VIII-IX: BADLY LAID PLANS

Lily receives her first cheque from Gus Trenor for a thousand dollars and attends a cousin's marriage where she again encounters the social set from the Trenors' summer home. There Trenor expresses irritation that she has not repaid him for his investments by spending more time with him. Lily fends him off with promises of a walk in the park and extricates herself from his company, but soon faces another difficult situation when Mr Rosedale intrudes on a conversation she is having with Selden. Acutely conscious of how Selden must perceive Lily's posturing before these wealthy gentlemen, Lily nearly insults Mr Rosedale but ultimately recoups the conversation and escorts the wealthier gentleman away.

Complications continue, however, several days later when Selden's maid mistakes Lily for his paramour and presents her with letters written to him by Bertha Dorset, with whom he is having an affair. Acutely conscious of how badly Selden would want the letters destroyed, Lily buys them from the maid and begins considering how to dispose of them before her aunt, Mrs Peniston, arrives home and interrupts her. Then, picturing Bertha Dorset smiling and "victorious" (p. 136), she seals them away in her wardrobe instead.

CHAPTERS X-XV: THE SITUATION WORSENS

Chapter X begins with a new social season that brings new trouble for Lily Bart. She attends the opera on the invitation of Mr Rosedale and is met by Gus Trenor's increasingly insistent claims on her attentions. Lily fends him off, but not before calling attention to herself, and rumours about her gambling and her flirtations gradually begin to circulate, even reaching her aunt when Miss Stepney mentions them in passing. Mrs Peniston is shocked at her niece's comportment but fails to confront or even discuss the matter with her, wanting to avoid a scene.

Endeavouring to restore her standing amongst her social set, Lily decides to join in on an evening of entertainment planned by the Dorsets for some newly acquired friends. Playing the titular role in a *tableau vivant* (cultural practice in which groups or individuals re-enact famous pieces of art) of Reynolds's *Mrs. Lloyd* (1775-1776), Lily attracts universal admiration for her beauty and poise. Deeply affected by what he feels to be "the whole tragedy of her life" (p. 162), Selden seeks her out after the show and declares his love for her. Lily seems to return his affections but leaves him in the garden, declaring "Ah, love me, love me—but don't tell me so!" (p. 165).

Receiving two notes the morning after the *tableaux vivants*, Lily sets off to the Trenors' city home, only to learn that Mr Trenor had deliberately invited her to call when his wife would be away. Trenor suggests that Lily owes him money and implies that she may already have been trading inappropriate favours with other men for money. Lily extricates herself from what becomes a frightening situation but is deeply shaken. Unable to return to her own home and her aunt's judgement, she turns to Gerty Farish for refuge.

Lily's situation only worsens the following morning when she confesses to her aunt the severity of her debts. The older woman chides her niece and agrees to cover the debt to the dressmaker but nothing else. Making Lily ever more vulnerable, she withdraws her support and declares the young woman "disgraced" (p. 202).

Waiting for Selden to call as promised in her second post-party note, Lily instead receives Mr Rosedale who makes a frank proposal of marriage to her. Insulted by his mention of her hardships, Lily dismisses the wealthy businessman and accepts an impromptu invitation by the ill-meaning Mrs Dorset. She leaves with them for the Mediterranean.

BOOK 2, CHAPTERS I-XIV: A LOVE STORY-TRAGEDY

The second Book of Wharton's novel finds Lily worse off than ever before. Returning home from disastrous travels with the Dorsets, Lily finds that she has fewer friends and options than before. Mr Rosedale renews his proposal that they enter into a mutually beneficial courtship and asks why Lily does not use Bertha Dorset's illicit letters to regain her social standing in that woman's circle, but Lily again refuses.

Desperate for money to pay her considerable debts, Lily moves out of the hotel in which she had been staying and takes up work first as the social secretary for a family new to New York society, then, once Bertha Dorset again besmirches her reputation, as secretary to a Mrs Hatch, and then in a milliner's shop. Devastated over her disgrace and beset by self-disgust, Lily becomes addicted to chloral hydrate. She overdoses the evening before Selden realises that he really does love her enough to attach his future to hers and plans to make her a proposal of marriage. He arrives the next morning to find Lily dead, receipts that prove she had finally settled all of her debts herself, and the city already moving on past the tragedy of her loss.

CHARACTER STUDY

LILY BART

The protagonist of Wharton's novel, Lily Bart is a beautiful and intelligent but shallow woman with a fondness for gambling and an aversion to budgeting. Born to wealthy parents, Lily 'came out' to society as a wealthy debutante but was soon after left destitute by her father's failed business ventures and his subsequent death. Travelling around Europe with her mother in the years after her father's death, Lily learns to despise her diminished financial standing and adopts her mother's obsession that she use her beauty to regain all that they had lost. Her mother dies on one of these frugal escapes abroad and Lily is taken in by her aunt with no further guidance other than her mother's advice that she use her beauty to win a great fortune through marriage.

At the beginning of *The House of Mirth*, Lily is already reaching the end of her most marriageable years and proves, by repeatedly sabotaging opportunities to wed wealthy men, that she is more romantic (like her father) than she had previously understood herself to be—she thinks she wants to marry solely for money but is unable to make herself do so, especially when Selden and the promise of love hover on the horizon.

LAWRENCE SELDEN

A lawyer of modest means who is nonetheless accepted by the highest ranks of New York society through long acquaintance, Selden is an old friend of Lily's and a source of stability in her life. Charmed by the advantages of extreme wealth, Selden nonetheless defines success through "personal freedom", namely freedom "from money, from poverty, from ease and anxiety, from all the material accidents" (p. 91). He loves Lily but realises too late that he could have saved her.

MRS JUDY TRENOR

Lily's best friend and the wife of Gus Trenor, Mrs Trenor endeavours to help her friend by putting her in the way of eligible and wealthy men like Percy Gryce.

MR GUS TRENOR

Judy Trenor's husband and a long-time acquaintance of Lily's, Gus Trenor uses the money he speculates on her behalf to make Lily feel indebted to him. Becoming increasingly demanding and threatening, Mr Trenor develops into a primary source of distress in Lily's life and contributes directly to her financial and social demise.

BERTHA DORSET

Lily's most explicit enemy, Bertha Dorset competes with Lily for the admiring attention paid to beautiful women. Having engaged in an extramarital affair with Selden, it is Bertha Dorset who wrote the letters Lily eventually saves from exposure. Unaware of the debt she owes her, Bertha Dorset spurns Lily's company and ruins the latter's reputation following their trip to the Mediterranean.

PERCY GRYCE

Lily's first chance at salvation, Percy Gryce is the wealthy but dull suitor scared off by rumours of Lily's gambling at the beginning of the novel. He marries Evie Van Osburgh instead.

GERTY FARISH

Gerty Farish is Selden's plain but practical cousin and the clearest foil for Lily's character in the novel. She lives alone, works, and is entirely independent. Gerty is a source of irritation for the novel's protagonist, not because of their differences but because, despite their differences and Gerty's plain appearance, she dares to be quite happy, and therefore represents the clearest argument in the novel against Lily's life and values. She is a grounding force in the novel as well as in Lily's life, and is the one person Lily is truly able to turn to in times of need.

MRS PENISTON

Mrs Peniston is the aunt who surprises the rest of their extended family by taking Lily in after the death of her mother. Generous but firm and far more practical than Lily, Mrs Peniston provides her niece with a comfortable life and allowance but refuses to pay her exorbitant debts when Lily's comportment proves disgraceful.

GRACE STEPNEY

Lily's cousin, much preferred by their aunt, Grace Stepney unwittingly exposes her cousin's gambling habits and failing reputation to their aunt with a passing reference.

MR SIMON ROSEDALE

A wealthy Jewish businessman, Mr Rosedale is a socially ambitious new arrival to Lily's world. He is largely scorned by Lily and her friends but so well-off that none dare to insult him. He makes two proposals of marriage to Lily, both of which she refuses.

ANALYSIS

MODERN MANNERS

Edith Wharton's *The House of Mirth* is often read as a novel of manners. Like Jane Austen's (English writer, 1775-1817) novels of the early 19th century, Wharton's 1905 publication depicts the intricate workings of a specific social set, in this case contemporary New York's social elite, in order to expose its hypocrisies and inner workings. Again like Austen, Wharton accomplishes this through her depiction of an intelligent young woman navigating her social position and, like Austen, Wharton succeeds because of her extreme talent at implementing irony and techniques of free indirect discourse. *The House of Mirth* does not lecture its reader on the excesses of upper-class New York; instead, it gradually reveals the hypocrisy and cruelty of the social strata it depicts by deftly exposing the differences between what its characters claim they value and how they behave.

Wharton's novel is therefore very much a novel of manners, but it is also a modern novel heavily influenced by the literary schools of Naturalism and Realism. The influence of Naturalism on Wharton's prose is particularly evident in the narrative's focus on fate and in its unflinching exploration of what might happen to a woman for whom things go badly. Indeed, just as the heroines of Gustave Flaubert (French writer, 1821-1880) or Thomas Hardy (English writer, 1840-1928), both giants of literary Naturalism, rarely escape their author's pages, Lily is doomed to what the narrator calls a "hateful" (p. 47) fate even from the early pages of her story. She never has any real means of saving herself and must either marry for money and subject herself to a life of boredom and subservience, or pass through the world as she does, precariously balanced between extreme indulgence and desperate poverty.

CLOTHES MAKE THE WOMAN

The society represented in Wharton's first major success is a highly superficial one predicated upon outward appearances above almost everything else. This society is particularly cruel to women, and while Wharton considers its negative impacts on men like Lily's father as well as the women in its pages, it is really the women who are shown to be most victimised by their society but also by themselves.

One of the ways in which Wharton shows the women of her novel to deconstruct themselves is their fixation on outward appearance. Lily is obsessed with her own beauty and with clothes, with their newness, their extravagance, and what they communicate to those around her. Her first troubles with money arise from debts owed to her dressmaker and it is partially out of a desire to continue receiving dresses as gifts from her friend that she first takes a seat at Mrs Trenor's gambling table.

The current design of her dresses has no real bearing on her physical or emotional wellbeing and yet, even when her practical aunt refuses to help her with any of her other debts, the older relative does commit to settle her dressmaker's bill: the costume of their rank is everywhere reinforced as a reasonable expense for what Selden calls "an artist" (p. 89) of their social set, like Lily.

THE BURDEN OF INTERIORITY

Despite the novel's emphasis on the importance of dressing well (i.e. expensively), Wharton's narrator constantly mediates between the external construction of a persona and true experience. Lily is constantly softening her features to endear herself to others or coyly sidestepping remarks to protect herself from precarious, even dangerous, situations with male interlocutors. When Trenor attacks her verbally in chapter XIII, Lily feels "suddenly weak and defenceless" (p. 173), but the narrator quickly notes the presence of "another self [...] sharpening her to vigilance" (*ibid.*).

Indeed, while Lily's mother considered her daughter's beauty to be "the last asset in their fortunes" (p. 55), Lily is more conscious of the role her talent for manipulation plays in her continued acceptance among their wealthy friends. Lily is constantly hiding her disdain or irritation behind admiring glances. She is a master manipulator as well as a great beauty.

Still, the very fact that the narrator so often remarks on Lily's awareness of her skill for manipulation or its implementation points towards the existence of another self, the true self which Selden observes she embodies "with a few people only" (p. 185). Gerty and Selden are two of the few characters privy to this true self, as Gerty herself remarks after the *tableau vivant*: "Don't you like her best in that simple dress? It makes her look like the real Lily—the Lily I know" (p. 163). The true Lily is only visible beneath the beauty of her clothes and makeup, beneath the mask of features she uses to charm the other actors in their social play of being friends and neighbours.

ABSURDITY AND MODERN TRAGEDY

The House of Mirth follows in a long tradition of narratives, written primarily by men, about female characters whose lives end tragically. Wharton's character is distinct from many of these other narratives, however, in that her character is not actually a 'fallen woman' (a term used to refer to women of a certain social strata who engage in intimate relations with men before marriage): she is only rumoured to be fallen. Lily's case is also distinct from many of these other depictions because of the number of vices to which she succumbs.

Indeed, Wharton does not just paint the portrait of a society which drives a young woman to destruction but also of a society which corners that young woman into destroying herself. In fact, each of her vices can be traced back to an external stressor: Lily first starts gambling to appease Judy Trenor and maintain her status among her friends; she turns to drug use to dull the pain of her loss of family, society, home, and status; even her tendency to tell people what they want to hear rather than what she truly thinks is born of an imperative need to keep powerful people on her side, to live off their fortunes even if those relationships make her disgusted with herself.

The insidiousness of these social pressures, the novel seems to suggest, cannot be resisted. Individuals must either succumb to their momentum or extricate themselves from their influence entirely, like Gerty Farish.

Because of this unflinching exploration of New York's elite society, Wharton's novel was extremely controversial and polarising when it was first published (Killoran, 2001: 25-26) and continues to elicit excited debate from readers and critics alike.

FURTHER REFLECTION

SOME QUESTIONS TO THINK ABOUT...

- What is the 'house of mirth'? What does its use as the title mean?
- Given the importance of clothes in this novel, what is the significance of the fact that Lily ends up working in a milliner's shop at her lowest point in the novel?
- Why does Selden arrive just after Lily has killed herself? Does this inopportune timing change the way we read the novel's ending? Can a story be simultaneously tragic and absurd?
- What role do Lily's parents play in the novel? In what ways does one or the other of her parents represent society? In what ways are they each reflected in Lily herself?
- Is Lily's death a suicide or an accident? What would the significance of either answer be?
- What role does self-sabotage play in Wharton's novel? In what way is Lily her own worst enemy? In what ways is she a victim?

- Why is it repeatedly remarked upon that Mr Rosedale is Jewish? Does this seem to be one of the reasons Lily and her friends drag their feet in welcoming him into their social circle? To what extent can this anti-Semitism be ascribed to the time in which Wharton was writing? How does this complicate or perhaps even enrich our reading of a novel aiming to expose the hypocrisies of the society it depicts?
- Describe Lily's interactions with the woman cleaning outside Selden's apartment. What do these interactions foreshadow? What do they tell us about social class during the time of Wharton's novel? What do they tell us about Lily's character?
- As mentioned above, the question of 'fate' comes up repeatedly in the novel. What role does 'fate' really play? Do you think the novel believes in 'fate'? Or is 'fate' just an excuse for bad choices?

We want to hear from you!
Leave a comment on your online library
and share your favourite books on social media!

FURTHER READING

REFERENCE EDITION

- Wharton, E. (1966) *The House of Mirth*. London, Constable and Company Ltd.

REFERENCE STUDIES

- Killoran, H. (2001) *The Critical Reception of Edith Wharton*. New York: Camden House.
- Lindberg, G. H. (1975) *Edith Wharton and the Novel of Manners*. Charlottesville: University of Virginia Press.
- Newlin, K. ed. (2011) *The Oxford Handbook of American Literary Naturalism*. Oxford: Oxford University Press.

ADDITIONAL SOURCES

- Lee, H. (2007) *Edith Wharton*. London: Chatto and Windus.
- Wharton, E. (1924) *The Writing of Fiction*. New York: Charles Scribner's Sons.

ADAPTATIONS

- *The House of Mirth*. (2000) [Film]. Terence Davies. Dir. USA: Sony Pictures Classics.

MORE FROM BRIGHTSUMMARIES.COM

- Reading guide – *The Age of Innocence* by Edith Wharton.

www.brightsummaries.com

Ebook EAN: 9782808017121

Paperback EAN: 9782808017138

Legal Deposit: D/2019/12603/23

Cover: © Primento

Digital conception by Primento, the digital partner of
publishers.